Simplicity with GOD
It's Now or Never
There Has Never Been a Time Like Now
to Partner with Your Creator
GOD
by
Lisa Lopez

Simplicity with GOD- It's Now or Never

There Has Never Been A Time Like Now to Partner with Your Creator
GOD

Copyright 2019 by Lisa Lopez

Introduction

It's times like these when people stop to think, what am I doing wrong? what am I doing right? And what should I do differently? If you're asking yourself those questions, then you're in the right place. This book is a guide to help you with those very questions.

It's the thick and thin of what you need to know to get aligned with not only your purpose but how to get there in the simplest terms.

The actions are as basic as you can get and still get where you want to be. So, buckle up and put on your saddle for the ride of your life.

Please understand this is not a book of how to live a good life, it's a book to show you how to live your best life. There is a difference. Think about how different night is from day and how each one shows you how to live. You learn how to be active by day and sleep by night well, so does this book. The difference is your day and night will be as clear as day. No more questions of self-doubt or if you are on the right path or not. If you are reading this book, you're probably still looking for the answer to that question and here you will find it.

How exciting that you will never have to look back and say," I never thought that I would be in this place of uncertainty again." Just like you want clarity, God wants that for you.

Welcome to "The Time is Now" so you "Never" have to be lost again.

Dedication

I would like to dedicate this book to all the people who:

Have taken the time to find and love God and all that comes with that.

The people who lead in a way that matters, no matter their circumstances.

The ones who if you ask about God, they can tell you. The children of God who make this world a better place and can show you how to be part of the Body of Christ.

Chapter 1
Why Are We Here?

It's never enough to think that you're just here for a moment. You are here for longer than you think. Your life as you know it is not what it really is. So, what is it? you might be asking. Well let's start with your job. It's the one thing you get to select. Everything else is determined by God, way before you ever arrived here. Now you certainly get to pick many options within your life also predetermined by God but nevertheless you are limited to what options God provides. Now don't panic, the options are mega.

Ever wonder why you go to work and then wonder why you are even there? It's because you are not where you're supposed to be. It is not what was agreed upon in the planning of your life. It's when you have gone astray and need to find your way back. Like being off path. Everything in your inner being is telling you to do something different but you keep doing what you're doing because you are comfortable or because you're dependent on the money. Well God has a surprise for you. It's not the money and never has been.

Money is a byproduct of doing what you are asked to do and that includes what God wants you to do. It is not a give and take, it's more like give and give back. So, let's go through an example:

If you get a dollar for taking care of your mom, would you not give that same dollar back for someone to take care of you? I am sure the answer is yes. So, this is how God works as it relates to money.

He gives you money to live, eat and sleep and you give back so others can live, eat and sleep. No matter the statue of that person. It's not your job to judge if someone should get a hamburger or not. It is your job to make sure they have one if they need one.

Now apply this to your current situation. Does it make sense for someone who needs food to not have any and there you are with an abundance? If the answer is yes, it makes sense. God needs you to re-evaluate why you feel that way and if the shoe was on the other foot, wouldn't you want someone to help you? Of course, you would want someone to help you, and that is exactly what will happen. If you feel like you are in a situation that requires you to hoard food in a time like this, you have an internal problem that only God can help you with. Seek his help.

Now if you answered no, it does not make any sense to have an abundance of food and not help others when they are in need, then you are on the right track. There is no simpler way to put it. What else does anyone need to say about it? There is nothing left to say. You either get it or you don't and if you don't, you will. One way or the other.

By that it means you can learn the easy way by what is being told to you through these words or by having to experience what it is like on the other end of that experience where food is not readily available. The choice is yours.

Why does that seem harsh, you might ask. It's not that it is harsh, but it is what is needed so your spirit is aligned to your creator. GOD.

So here is where God is going with this. He wants everyone to help each other the way life was intended to be lived and not the other way around where you only help those who you think need help.

If you see a need and you can fulfill it. DO IT!

Here is another example just in case you're not clear by now:
If you had one dollar and God took it from you. You would think he was mean, but if you gave it to God, you would feel good about it right? Well of course you would, because when you give, you give to God and when he takes, he still gives to you. Now what he will give you is a lesson on how to give and give from the heart because you will know what it feels like to have something taken away from you. So, everybody wins whether you see it or not. It's the way life works.

Evaluate your current situation and see how this applies to you if at all. If it does, then make the change. If it does not, then you're on the right track. I am sure by now things are getting crystal clear for you.

Let's say at a minimum that you are trying your best to help where help is needed, and you still want to do more. Then you can pray. Prayer provides for people just like God does. God makes sure that your prayers are answered and be sure you say "In Jesus Name, Amen" at the end of every prayer. It's required to move the prayer upward.

If you keep your eyes on the prize, which is being able to be part of the solution and not part of the problem things will turn around quickly.

Go in peace and be a peace provider.

This is why you are here.

Chapter 2
Who Do You Think You Are?

If you are ever wondering who you are, well let's talk about that. I am sure that God has come up with a way for you to be who you want to be but also be who he wants you to be. Together with God is how you figure that out. You will always wonder until you don't and that's when you know, you know God.

There are no questions that go unanswered when you know God. He not only answers all your questions, but he makes them clear to you in more ways than one. He will talk to you, show you visions, bring people into your life that show you and tell you things, and many other ways. Either way the message will be clear.

Who you are is primarily up to God but your deliverance of that is up to you? Let's go through an example:
If you decide to be a lawyer, then that's great and God will do everything you need him to do so that you are successful. In return he expects for you to make the outcomes of your cases the best example of *fair* and *just* in the best interest of the people.

He does not want you to do something to help someone who is lying and cheating the system. This is not only a degradation to the process but also to the ones who are doing the right thing. In other words, do the right thing and do it often.

It's in your hand to choose who you help and how you help them so when presented with the choice, choose wisely. If you don't, the not so wise case will come back as a mark against you in the tallies of heaven. What does that mean? It means you must now repent and ask for forgiveness for your actions. Once you are forgiven, which you have been by Jesus, you must then change your ways. It's a shot you get time and time again. The thing to remember is every time you repeat your offense it will be released into your life as an experience that causes hardship because of the hardships you caused others.

Now I am sure you have heard of the saying "In everything, do to others as you would have them do to you". If you have not, then it's time you read about it in Mathew 7:12. The bible that is. That's the book with all the power tools you need for the game of life. Get one and read it.

Every now and then you will see how others come into your life and cause to think about something differently and those people are heaven sent. They are the providers that we talked about in the previous chapter. These people are sent to you for a reason. They help you get your roadmap right and try to get you on the right path to ease your journey based on the direction God has given them.

Just like you now, are getting the words from God through someone you have probably never heard of. A doer of God's kingdom and providing for you in his service.

You are who God says you are. You are the children of God who come from his kingdom and live in a place that requires love, compassion, and ministry. Keep your eyes open for the signs of the times so you are prepared to help when God needs your help. Yes, there is preparation that is required and here is what that entails:

First, educating yourself about God is preferred but not required at this stage. It certainly makes things easier. The way you get educated is by reading the Bible and asking questions that you want answered. You can do this by praying, writing down or asking the wise ones in your life.

Next you are required to make sure that what you are working on is a project for the people. By this, it means to make sure you are helping others in a way that matters.

Here are few ideas just to name a few:

- Feed the hungry
- Show love to others
- Make a bed available to those who don't have one
- Keep your eyes out for people who prefer to keep you in a negative way, influencers of sin/wrongdoing. By the way- never ask for forgiveness if you're not sorry for what you have done otherwise it won't matter what you say it only matters what you do.

- Seek your own destiny not the destiny of others (You were born alone, and you will die alone) so what does it matter what others say or think about your show. It's not like tickets are for sale.

- Be simple minded towards your interactions with God as no matter what you are his child. In other words, don't feel like you are not smart enough or religious enough to talk to God. He listens to your heart not your mind.

- Take time to enjoy what is around you. Look at the world as a playground for you and take care of it.

- The trees and flowers are there for your enjoyment not for your pleasure. Leave them alone unless they serve a helpful purpose.

- Keep your waters clean of pollution and trash as it's the only water you have. Remember how quickly it can be taken away if not appreciated. Do your part.

- Watch for the children around you as everyone who is a parent is a parent to all kids. Anyone who is a mother or father is one to all as well. It's not a one for one title, it's a one for all position.

Time is of the essence so see where you can help and HELP! It's the action that counts not the thought of the action. We need doers of the dream not dreams of the doers. This is who you are.

Chapter 3
It's Now or Never

Why is it now or never? It's now or never because if you ever select to do nothing and wait until the last minute, there will be no tomorrow.

It's wonderful for you to think and care if the choices you make, really make a difference? This way you never underestimate your actions.

Keep yourself out of harm's way and know you are protected. If ever in doubt just ask your main protector who in case, you're not aware is Jesus Christ.

Now Jesus came to help you in a way that no one else can. His mission here is to save you from an unknown destiny and make sure that you align with God's will. He does that in many ways.

One of his main purposes is to make sure that no matter what you've done wrong in this life you are forgiven. God hands you over to him for some time while this alignment occurs. What really happens is Jesus takes the wheel. He takes everything you have done and divides it into sections. Looking at what you've done well, where you need improvement, and the condition of your heart. He never judges you. He only looks at ways to make you better and he exposes those areas to you one at a time.

For example: These are things like how you handle yourself when you're angry, when do you decide if you're right or wrong, things you do out of jealousy. All of these behaviors are things of importance when it comes to how you would align to God's will.

It's the highway to Heaven for example: Jesus holds the keys to the kingdom and now he wants to give them to you.

The only way he can do that is for you to prove that you're worthy of them. What does worthy look like? What does that mean you might be asking? Here's the answer.

You have to know who you're dealing with when it comes to God. Jesus knows better than anyone that's why he's your teacher, protector, and guide. Following Jesus is like following the yellow brick road. Leading you to the Real Wizard of Oz. Now along the path Jesus gives you help, and those helpers make sure you learn what's required for you to learn to move forward. Those helpers are things like Spirit Guides, Angels, and the Holy Spirit. All of which you will get to know on your journey.

So, here's how you get started:

First you turn to God and ask him for help on how to pray, and he will grant you that. Asking for help on how to pray nudges the Holy Spirit to now pay attention because you're ready to activate and use the Holy Spirit. This has been given to you and truly lives inside of you.

Once that prayer is complete it will be granted to you immediately and this allows the Holy Spirit to help you pray even if you don't know how. A real GODSEND for praying as you move forward.

The next thing that you will do is in your prayer you will ask Jesus to come into your heart to be your teacher, your protector, and your savior. Then you will say in Jesus' name. Amen.

Once you have done that now just believe and wait. Jesus is now available for your every need.

Keep him close to you as everything you need to know will be provided one way or the other. He will ask what you need, he will determine the best way for you to have that and he will never try to change you. He will only show you a better way. GOD's way.

Let's look at an example:
If you say, "God, I want you in my life". Jesus will say, "here are the things that you need to do one at a time." He will say. "Come to me with all your problems and let me show you how to solve them."

Now this can be tricky because the solutions may require you to take action. He will only require action that moves you into the best part of yourself. Which really means exiting out negativity that's been stored away in your heart.

He may ask you to repent and change your ways about certain activities or actions, he may ask you to make amends with people that you are in disagreement with. You may be asked to give a blessing to someone today that you might have anger towards. At the end of it all, it's cleaning your heart. A pure heart is what is required to interact directly with God.

Now you can choose to interact with God without Jesus, but given all that he has to offer, and his purpose here why would you not choose him? Think about it, if someone has paid the price for your sins, made sure that your illnesses and pain have already been felt, why would you not take advantage of that. It goes back to the question of how easy or hard you want your life here to be.

So, keep in mind half of the work required by you has already been done by Jesus. Here's the difference by way of an example:

If you decide to hurt someone and then afterwards you feel bad about it, you're going to have to ask for forgiveness. Having Jesus in your life you have already been forgiven. Without Jesus in your life, **you** will have to pay the price. It's the difference between living by the Old Testament pre-Jesus or the New Testament with Jesus.

If you have to pay the price it could cost you your life, like the days of various Kings. If you haven't read the Old Testament, the message of it is the way life was, an eye for an eye type of life. Now this does not mean that God is going to kill you or take your eyeball, what this means is that you will have struggles in your life that are unnecessary. Those struggles provide the experience and the repentance that's required for that act of negativity. So, the choice is yours. Choose Wisely.

The reason it's now or never is because if you don't act now, you probably never will. If the ultimate goal is aligning to God's will, I guarantee you now is better than never. Why take chances that have risk when you have a solution that is guaranteed. Even your smartest investors would recommend that. Consider yourself advised.

Chapter 4
Here's What You Need to Know

Just like when you need to know if something is true or not, you typically ask a friend. Well now you have access to the one and only source of Truth and that is God through Jesus. Now while not all truth is accepted right away. It's a matter of one's beliefs. Meaning what you believe is what you get.

Let's look at beliefs via an example:
If you believe the tree grows from its roots you would be correct.

If you believe the roots of a tree are the roots of evil, would still be correct. Now why on Earth would I give an example like that?

Because in both situations it's what you believe that matters. Believing in something good is better than believing in nothing. When you believe in nothing you get nothing. When you believe in something good, you get something good. On the opposite side if you believe in something bad you will get something bad.

I wonder why you would ever want to think bad things unless you feel like you're not worthy of good things, which for a lot of people that may be true in their own head.

But it's the farthest from the truth. God never intended for you to suffer with hardships however, given the signs of the time it's inevitable to be in a place that requires your attention. This means it's time for you to understand that you are worthy of love and to bring yourself back into alignment with God where you were originally created.

If you think you're here on accident reading this information, you would be mistaken. This book is intended for the exact audience that requires this information at the time they need it. Deliverance is what that is called. Another act of kindness from your loving father.

So, here's what you need to know:

> ➢ Come to God with all your heart using Jesus as your guide.
> ➢ Do it now and save yourself unsatisfactory time.
> ➢ Keep going in your ways of error and see the sadness grow.
> ➢ Change your heart forevermore and be the one who sows.
> ➢ Distinction is of silliness so let it go by the wayside.
> ➢ You are only "What God Says You Are" so let go of your pride.
> ➢ It starts with what you believe in, but it ends with God's final plan.

Chapter 5
It's Better Than You Think

What's better than you think? Well, it's your perception of what is really going on in the world around you. It's God.

Here is the thick and thin of it all.

If you try to pick a place in this world that is not under God's jurisdiction, you would never be correct. It's all God. God is everything and in everyone no matter the race, color, political view, or any other prejudice you have come up with in your own minds. So, think about it this way: If you come to me and say God, how did I get here? God would tell you, I put you here with the help of your parents. Then of course you will ask Why? God would tell you because I needed you here to help me save this world. How? By keeping your faith that was provided to you which allows you to always work with me. Using your faith, you would be asked to do things in this world that make it a better place. That is the bottom line.

There is no magical formula that so many people are trying to figure out. No ceremonies required to talk to God. Just you and God utilizing Jesus and his helpers. That's It! That's the winning combination to Life's Lottery! Those 6 numbers you keep trying to win for a dollar are only a figment of your imagination and not sustainable. So put your money where your mouth is and use that dollar to feed somebody who needs to eat, and watch the favor come back to you many times over.

So now you know the secret that is not even a secret so gossip away about that and not your fellow brothers and sisters. How this has gotten out of control. The hate and envy of one person to another and why? Are we not all in this together? Well, we are whether you know it or not. I am sure this is the reality of what you are seeing the world today with the universal virus of Covid-19. Keep yourself safe in the comfort of your own homes. It's the best place for you to find God.

Here are a few tips:
- Check your level of stress and reduce it.
- Keep yourself clean of toxins both internal and external.
- Never ask for something you already have. This means if you have food don't ask for it again or it can be taken away from you. Why? Because if you knew what it felt like to have no food, you would be thankful for the food you do have. Make sense?
- Hoarding is a sin in so many ways. If you have, share. If you don't have to ask for your share through grace provided by God.
- Adjust your vision to align with what is in front of you not what is behind you. Let go of the past and focus on the now.
- It's great to have a vision of where you want to go but you need to focus on what you're doing now that will get you there.
- Information overload is never productive, go with the flow of energy that is inside of you and not with the TV roadshow. It can be a circus of information

that can keep you confused. You have all the answers already inside of you. Go to that channel with your inward breathing and not the TV remote.

- Pace yourself at an enjoyable rate since the stress of it all is more that you can take. You're not designed to carry the load, only God is. Let him.
- See how much better it is.

Chapter 6
Supreme Beings

Extra Terrestrial activity is a thing of the past. It's the future that you should be concerned about. It's not the aliens you are chasing that matter. It's the apocalypse. No not the end of the world event, but the near to the world event. I am sure you are asking by now what on earth am I talking about? Well, it goes like this:

If you take a minute out of your day to say a prayer and God does not respond immediately, you think it's the end of the world. But God looks at it like a diamond in the rough. He sees someone who really needs something and is coming to him for help. Yet all you see is a prayer unanswered. What do you think is more important? I am sure you think your prayer unanswered is more important because you are focused on yourself. What if God did that? What if God's only focus was himself/herself? It would really be a shocker if the only prayers that were answered were of his own. Well guess what? In either case the prayers would get answered. Why? Because you are a mini-God. You are a human form of God. When you focus on that part of yourself you get the same results as if you went to God, because you are God too. A mini version in human form.

Let's be clear about one thing, you will not be able to change the world with your breath like God did, but you can certainly change the world for the better.

This is what Supreme Beings do. They focus on themselves first and then they put goodness out into the world. Now how do you become a Supreme Being?

Here are the steps to success:
First, you come to God and ask for his help to be a person of interest. Once you have done that you are in. Not sure how to ask? Here is how:
- Take your head and bow it.
- Lift your arms and say." God, I am the person you want me to be. Thank you for your guidance and deliverance. In Jesus Name, Amen.

When you say it like you mean it, it sounds great but it's not until you mean it does it count. Going through the motions for the wrong reasons is as effective as a spec of pollen that you can't even see but you know is there. Don't waste your time with fake or pretend vocabulary. It won't work. It just won't. Instead start to say to yourself, "I matter, I am a child of God" and before you know it, you will be, and the rest is history.

Now about those aliens....Just kidding.

Chapter 7
Super Realism- The Reality Check

Now of course you want to know what the difference between super realism and your current reality is.

Here is the difference. It's the way the world works, as the world turns you might say. Let's look at an example: When little Tommy told his mom he really wanted a puppy for Christmas, and he then received one. What do you think really happened? How do you think he received that puppy? Well, it was not Santa Clause unless that's what you want to call it. Like many do. It was the power of prayer that that child provided during his ask. Your child says" I want a puppy for Christmas" and he received one. So, think about this. If you are also a child of God, do you really think he would not give you what you ask for? Well, he does as long as it serves a good purpose. He will even give you something that you don't like if it serves a good purpose.

Many of you require a few out-of-pocket experiences in order for you to see how deep your pockets really are in God. If you learn from them, the cost is well worth it. If you don't your spending habits are on the rise until you do.

You will spend on things that don't make a difference one way or the other. Material things will sit and collect dust while all along they were not meant to help you.

What does help you? Where should you focus when you want something? You focus on God. You tell him what you want, and he will decide if you're going to receive it as a form of GRACE or even MERCY. Both are considered gifts from God to his children. If you get it. You're on the right track with what you're asking for. If you, don't it is ok. You will soon enough.

So where do you go from here? You go to God, tell him what you want and believe you will get it. There is no trick or magic to this statement. It means exactly what it says. Ask and you shall receive as long as you believe.

That is the meaning of super realism. It's the real of it all.

Chapter 8
The End of Times

The end of times is not what you think it is. It's not the end of the world, it's only the end as you know it today. There is a whole other world out there waiting for you to arrive. I am not talking about another planet like Mars, I am talking about a world of peace and harmony. One that you are in charge of day in and day out. God calls it "Heaven on Earth"; it's your ultimate goal of life. When you get to that goal, it's like the Heavens have opened and a wealth of knowledge comes rushing out for you. It is the answer to all your questions like you never knew before. I mean a waterfall of events, clarity, discussion with your creator, and meaningful living but living in peace no matter the situation. It's what is waiting for you and has been all your life.

Consider this to be the light at the end of the tunnel and the bells of your own church.

Just think how many times you decided to keep doing things the way you are and how many times you keep coming back to square one and having to start over. Well, this is not that. This is a one-way path to your destiny and the family that got you there.

So, let's get down to the nitty gritty of this and clear this up as clear as it can be.

When you come down from heaven to earth and then you make the bed you lie in the best way you can. You do this alone. When you learn about how God is your creator you then decide to remake your bed with clean sheets and clean pillowcases. The old ones do not make you happy anymore. This is what God is talking about. He makes your new bed a place more comfortable and a place of honor just for you.

He always makes you the focus of his attention and predetermines who will keep you company 24 hours a day. It may be an angel, or a spirit guide or even Jesus but you are always accompanied by one of God's helpers. At some point you also become one of God's helpers and that is how God gets his mission accomplished in this universe. By allowing you to play a part in his movie within the Universal Studio.

I hope by now the truth has resonated within you and you are on your way to being who God created you to be.

Go in peace.

Acknowledgement

GOD is Real Poem

If God is real, then so are you

Try asking if that is the real truth

Keeping your heart open is the way to learn

That nothing else matters not even the earth

Water and Land keep things afloat

So why do you insist on rocking the boat

Stability is found

Of sound mind and body

So stabilize your heart and the rest will follow

Jesus is the way, keep him near

Follow his lead for the best outcome

Near and Dear

About the Author

Lisa Lopez

A mother of two and a grandmother of four. Lisa Lopez is a published author of:

- Coping with Landau-Kleffner Syndrome, A Family Story a personal family battle that she shares to help others who need help with this debilitating disorder.
- Simplicity with GOD, Simple Steps from Beginner's Faith to a Daily Friendship with GOD.
- Simplicity with GOD- Effortless Devotions- Rapid Read

Professionally, Lopez has 30 years' experience in the Financial Services Industry and a passion for helping others. She volunteers for multiple hunger programs and mentors' veterans who want to rejoin corporate America. Lopez was born in 1966 in Houston, TX where she still currently resides.

Thank You for Reading My Book!

May GOD Bless You!!

In His Service

Lisa Lopez Lopezfaith0731@gmail.com

Simplicity with GOD Community Facebook

https://www.facebook.com/groups/486209585505895

https://www.facebook.com/Lopezfaithcoach

www.ingramcontent.com/pod-product-compliance
Lightning Source LLC
Chambersburg PA
CBHW071807020426
42331CB00008B/2424